JO: Art of the Japanese Short Staff
by Dave Lowry

Editor: Mike Lee
Graphic Design: Sergio Onaga
Graphic Assistant: Jeanne Thomas

© 1987 Ohara Publications, Inc.
All rights reserved
Printed in the United States of America
Library of Congress Catalog Card Number: 87-42877
ISBN 0-89750-116-0

Eleventh Printing 2004

WARNING

BLACK BELT BOOKS
A Division of **OHARA ⑩ PUBLICATIONS, INC.**
World Leader in Martial Arts Publications

JO: Art of the Japanese Short Staff

by Dave Lowry

Acknowledgements

On extremely abbreviated notice, Michael Belzer of Shindo Muso-ryu and Hombu aikido, served as my partner for the illustrations. His advice, cooperation, and skills were invaluable.

Thanks too, to Mr. Lough and Ms. Chalfant, and to all the others at the aikido dojo who were patient and uncomplaining *uke*.

Foreword

As the reader goes through this book he will encounter a substantial amount of Japanese terminology. A glossary is provided to assist. The jo however, is like all the budo, firmly embedded in traditional Japanese culture. To strip its training of the language in which it was created is to deny its roots and so to take a major step in perverting it.

A more empirical reason for the Japanese words is this: the serious student need not go far in his practice before he finds himself among Japanese speaking instructors. Familiarity with the basic terminology will not only facilitate training, it may play a vital role in the student's safety.   —D.L.

About the Author

Dave Lowry belongs to the 21st generation of the Yagyu Shinkage-ryu, one of the most venerated of the classical Japanese martial schools, with a close connection to Zen and the politics of feudal Japan. His training began in 1968 under the tutelage of Ryokichi Kotaro of Nara Prefecture, Japan. The unbroken lineage of the Yagyu Shinkage-ryu of which he is part includes several warriors of note: Yagyu Muneyoshi, who founded the ryu in the 16th century; Yagyu Toshiyori, first headmaster of Owari Yagyu Shinkage-ryu; Matsunaga Keinosuke, who participated in the battle of Sekigahara as a retainer of the Lord Miyoshi; Osada Itaro, teacher of fencing and tea ceremony to the sixth shogun, Tokugawa Yoshimune; and Okimoto Shuzo, retainer and assistant to the *fudai* (principal lord), Matsudaira Keiei.

Lowry's martial arts training also encompasses several of the modern budo disciplines. He was tutored in the art of *aiki-jo* (the stick art of aikido) by Yutaka Funaki and Sachiyo Fujii, both expert teachers of hombu aikido, and has also trained extensively in Kodokan judo and karate-do. Lowry, who is the author of *Bokken, The Art of the Japanese Sword* (Ohara Publications), lives and trains near St. Louis, Missouri.

Preface

The jo is an exceptional weapon in that, unlike the sword, *naginata* (halberd), or the other finely wrought arms of the professional military class of old Japan, it is the lowliest of all tools—an ordinary length of wood. We do not speak of famous jo made by master smiths the way we do of the *katana* (long sword). But the jo can and has snapped the best sword blades ever forged. In old Japan it could be carried by the poorest peasant—even the mighty Tokugawa regime couldn't very well outlaw a stick in a commoner's hands—yet at least one school of the jo bears the noble appellation *Tenshin Sho* (inspired by divine instruction).

The aspiring student of the jo might be baffled at the extensive range of methods, traditional schools *(ryu),* and techniques available to him in Japan. Most notably, the jo is taught as a classical budo discipline. Its applications against the Japanese sword are the basis of Shindo Muso-ryu and numerous offshoots of that school of jo. Many of these older *ko-ryu* (classical weapons arts) contain within their field of study jo techniques which involve trapping, striking, and manipulating the jo as a fulcrum to perform devastating throws and joint locks. The techniques in this book are not a guide to Shindo Muso-ryu. The jo of the Shindo Muso-ryu and various jo federations is an example of the classical budo. It is practiced and taught in clubs in dozens of nations and, closely regulated, its standards are high.

A largely distinct version of the jo can be found within the styles of aikido, which instruct a method of using the weapon best described as *aiki-jo,* in complement to the circular, flowing techniques of aikido. The techniques presented in this book are those of aiki-jo. They follow closely the approach taken for teaching the jo to upper level aikido students. Morihei Uyehshiba, the founder of aikido, distilled many of them from the ways of using the spear and in principle they resemble closely movements of the spear and naginata.

All of these methods differ radically and they should not be confused with one another, though all are part of the combative schema of Japan's professional warrior class.

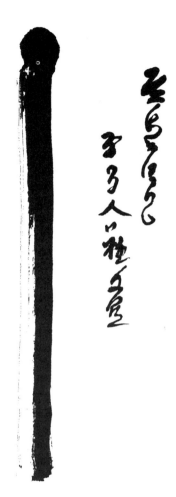

Introduction

When the budo were confined to the boundaries of Japan and practiced solely by members of its societal and cultural groups, few problems of misinterpretation occurred. Since the martial Ways had been derived from combative arts that existed in Japan for centuries, they were not a foreign influence but an integral part of the life-style. In that setting, the aspiring budoka who wished to learn an art of the jo knew reasonably well what he was getting into. He had few false perceptions and invariably allowed his teachers and seniors to guide him toward an ever-maturing understanding.

When the budo were transplanted to other cultures, however, a proper and true perspective of them was not always instilled. Foreign cultures introduced to the Japanese budo may have had their own combative traditions and warrior values, usually distinct from or in contrast to those of the budo's native clime. And unless the teacher was extremely careful or skilled with an ability to communicate, his *do* form could suffer from misinterpretations by non-Japanese students. These misconceptions can be in turn, disastrous and amusing. In Great Britain, for instance, with its long history of knighthood and chivalry, many aspiring budoka quite naturally and quite erroneously assumed the samurai and his code of *bushido* were merely Eastern counterparts to their Arthurian traditions. Happily myopic, these sorts continue to affix to their practice of the budo, all sorts of values and historical perspectives utterly alien to it. In the United States, some of the first immigrant karate sensei decided, unwisely in retrospect, to demonstrate the power of their art by breaking planks of wood at public exhibitions. Disregarding the sensei's acknowledgement that these stunts were only peripherally connected with the real goals of karate-do, untold legions of the Machismo Majority eagerly seized upon this practice and have been determinedly setting about deforesting entire lumberyards ever since.

As the jo becomes more and more popular within martial arts circles in countries outside Japan, the potential increases that it will be similarly misinterpreted. And rapidly following upon misinterpretation is misdirection, with students trailing off upon roads of jo training that lead to nowhere. In the hopes of forestalling that, it is imperative to begin on the correct course.

The use of the jo, like the weapons and methods of all the budo, has been directed for many years now to the self-perfection of the participant and not to the destruction of another human being. It will be regrettable step backward if this evolving process is allowed to degenerate into another form of fighting. The student of the jo must always keep in mind that his weapon is taken from a combative art and his bearing and concentration must reflect that attitude as well. Yet, it is to train in the forms of combat and not in their practical application or execution that the budoka should direct his efforts. A perfect example is the *tandoku renshu* (short solo exercise) presented in this book.

Within any tandoku renshu, or any kata, lie a wealth of techniques and lessons that all too often go unmined by modern exponents. The 31-count tandoku renshu of the jo is no exception. Contained in it are methods of shifting the body, attacking with strikes or different pinning and throwing techniques. It is fair to say, in fact, that a resolute study of even a simple exercise like this one could well be a decade's worth of investigation and effort. The purposes of this book then, are to provide some basic information on the methods of holding, striking and moving with the jo, to illustrate and explain an uncomplicated and common tandoku renshu that employs most of those fundamentals and, most importantly, to provide a detailed explanation and analysis of the meaning behind the exercise.

This kind of analysis is known as *bunkai*, a much neglected form of study within the budo. For the budoka who reads of masters in the old days who practiced only one or two kata during their entire lives, the inevitable question is "Didn't that get boring?" And the answer is, no, it didn't, because of bunkai. As the exponent progresses, from the moment of his introduction to a kata or exercise until he has practiced it for nearly a lifetime, he will constantly be exposed to deeper and more complex meanings behind its outward form.

A word of warning about bunkai is appropriate here. In the tandoku renshu included in this book, a number of bunkai are explained and illustrated. These, however, should in no way be considered a complete analysis of the exercise. As one continues to practice under the guidance of a competent teacher the movements will seem to constantly change before his eyes, taking on new meanings as he delves further and further into their multi-faced nature. The bunkai here are intended to demonstrate that the kata or tandoku renshu of an art can have many more meanings than those which are immediately visible. But this is only an introduction. For the practitioner to really enter into the deeper strata of bunkai, he must apprentice himself to a worthy teacher. And he must practice, practice, practice.

Contents

WHY TRAIN WITH THE JO?

Presently, while there is a significant interest in the arts and Ways of Japan, we stand at an expanding distance from the era of the warriors who cultivated those disciplines. It can be difficult, equipped as we are with 20th-century sensibilities, for modern budoka to accurately grasp the essence of the spirit that animated the classical warrior, the *bugeisha,* who flourished in Japan from the first part of the 15th century until the twilight of feudalism late in the 19th. Given this great cultural gap, the modern student is plagued by tendencies to romanticize, underestimate or otherwise misinterpret the ethos of the bugeisha, or to ascribe to him the values and concepts of a modern age. Gross distortions can be inculcated in the minds of those who believe they are carrying on that spirit, and the modern budoka may come to consider himself a contemporary incarnation of the classical bugeisha.

This conception is almost totally errant, even from a purely technical point of view. The modern budoka nearly always directs his practice toward goals of personal defense in non-military circumstances such as streetside encounters, or other kinds of personal assaults for instance, or as a means of recreation or sport. Techniques emphasized then, are those which will disable an assailant or which will score a point. The techniques of the classical bugeisha, however, were directed entirely to the defense of his clan or that of his lord's. The concept of self, as in "self-defense," was understood to be the collective self of the group *(dantai)* and it was toward protection of this unit that the bugeisha was trained to conduct his combative efforts. Further, since his encounters were nearly always against social equals—other professional warriors—his methods had to be instantaneously and irreversibly conclusive. There was no opportunity to stun or temporarily halt an opponent. The battle had to be begun and finished in an instant, and was immediately lethal to one participant or both. The idea of merely disarming or partially incapacitating his enemy was not a very important part of the classical bugeisha's strategy. The notion of trying to score a point in some sporting manner occurred to him not at all.

More vitally, the singular distinction between the classical bugeisha and his modern counterpart may be measured in terms of the spirit. For the bugeisha, training was not a matter of spending a few hours a week polishing his craft. He entered into it as a lifelong pursuit. He maintained a steadily receptive frame of mind, constantly instilling within himself an attitude of alertness, incessantly assessing and evaluating situations and reacting accordingly. For him the physical confrontations of the *dojo* also imparted lessons in personal comportment that could be, and were, applied to daily life. The strategy of the classical martial arts was therefore mirrored in his manners and in the way he conducted himself in society.

Today it is the rare budoka indeed who approaches his budo with such a spirit. The constraints of time, the responsibilities needing our attention, and more honestly, the distractions competing for it, are major obstacles. The modern budoka should, however, make every attempt to study his *do* with the same dedication the bugeisha approached his art. The more deeply and fully he attends to whatever form of martial Way he has choosen, the greater understanding and appreciation he is bound to have for it. The *do,* when approached with this intensity, arise as something more than physical exercise: it emerges as it was truly meant to be, a Way for life, in all its facets and aspects, to be lived fully and honestly.

While there are many avenues to this more profound approach to the budo, one of the best is to take up the art of one of the traditional weapons of old Japan.

The modified or contrived implements produced nowadays as self-defense aids, or sporting derivatives such as the bamboo *shinai* or *naginata,* are insufficient for such a purpose. Rather, the modern budoka should take up those arms that were employed by the bugeisha in actual combat or in his training. The modern budoka may wonder at this insistence, especially if his chosen *do* form is concerned primarily with empty-handed methods. But as soon as he commits himself to a serious practice with a weapon, he will begin to see a wealth of value in it. Relatively inexpensive, easily acquired and maintained, the jo is an excellent example of one such weapon the budoka might consider.

With a weapon like the jo in his hands, the budoka is suddenly faced with all sorts of details, most of which he never before considered. How does he carry it safely in the dojo? How should he bow and move around with it when not actually training? What kind of distance is necessary for the jo to be effective? All of these questions (which he may have neglected to ask in training empty handed) suddenly add new significance to the fundamentals of his art. Engaged in practice, a similarly beneficial situation arises. With the jo, the student soon becomes absorbed with problems of the weapon's trajectory, the exact location of its targets, correct intervals; all things he often overlooks in his regular training. Practice with the jo brings him face to face with these considerations and causes him to investigate their importance at a more intense level than he otherwise might.

Then too, there is a certain undeniable seriousness that enters the dojo when a weapon is in use there. This alone is ample rationale for jo training. If the budo are not perceived and pursued as a means of *seishi o choetsu* (confronting the fear of life and death), then they are reduced to the level of an inconsequential exercise. Although it should be obvious that every precaution be taken and danger avoided, the possibility of danger is absolutely crucial to the education of the budoka. He must face the critical realization that a mistake on his part or his partner's, unlike errors made in sports, cannot be "fixed" with a "whoops, sorry." Even a fractional miscalculation made with the jo, whether one is attacking or receiving an attack, can be fatal. Such a realization will hone his reflexes and his spirit, and bring the budoka to a more solid comprehension of what the budo are all about.

With a jo in his grip, the budoka can begin to gain some sense of the values and life-style of the classical bugeisha that preceded him. He is enabled at the same time to achieve a greater awareness of the fullest goals of his modern budo, and of the responsibilities and power that are inherent within all of them. The practice of the jo spans the entire epoch of the traditional Japanese martial arts and Ways, from the time of the ancient warriors until the present.

EVOLUTION OF CLASSICAL JOJUTSU

When one considers it is really only a short, round stick of wood, it is even more intriguing to ponder what an elemental gap the hardwood jo has filled in the history and evolution of the martial disciplines of Japan. The long sword or *katana,* was the central arm of the Japanese warrior throughout most of his reign, and is undoubtedly the most highly developed in its application. The spear, dipped, according to Japanese mythology, into the vast misted emptiness of space by a primeval god and lifted out to drip from its point the droplets of firmament that became the islands of Japan, has almost a religious connotation attached to it. And the bo, or long wooden staff, is the most archaic of weaponry in Japan. In comparison, the humble jo seems quite plebian. And yet, the jo possesses many of the attributes of all three of these revered arms: the slashing stroke of the katana, the thrusting reach of the spear, and the reversible striking power and indestructibility of the bo. It is little surprise that, for all its simplicity, once its development began, a forest of schools and masters soon sprang up to further refine and perfect the jo as a formidable weapon.

To trace the history of the short stick in combat in Japan would be an impossible task, dating as it must, from the moment a prehistoric aborigine there snatched up a piece of dead wood to use. In Japan, with its many oak and cedar forests, this opportunity must have come early and often. There is no evidence, however, of a systematized method of combat with the short wooden staff until the Muromachi era (1336-1600), when the rapidly developing samurai class began to incorporate it into the first of the traditional ryu.

When the samurai wielded the wooden staff, though, he chose almost exclusively the bo, a weapon of between five and seven feet in length, virtually ignoring any kind of shorter stick weapon. Just why the jo was neglected is a mystery, although some guesses can be ventured. First, the length of the bo made it an extremely effective polearm against other long weapons like the spear and naginata, both of which were in popular use at that time. In fact, in many schools of classical bujutsu the bo is gripped and manipulated in a manner very similar to techniques with those two weapons.

Early ryu which maintained bojutsu in their curriculum included the

Katori Shinto-, the Kashima Shinto-, and the Takenouchi-ryu. Their *waza* emphasized the length of the bo, striking from a distant range or using the bo as a fulcrum, swinging it at a terrific speed that could shatter bones as well as the strongest steel sword. By the end of the feudal era it is estimated that over 300 ryu had made bojutsu a part of their training, and even those bugeisha from styles which did not feature the bo were made familiar with its employment and the best defenses against it.

The typical bo usually labeled a *rokushakubo,* measured about six feet in length, which must be compared to the average height of the Japanese male at that time, more than a foot shorter. "Rokushaku" denotes a measurement: a *shaku* is roughly equal to the American foot, and *roku* is "six." The weapon was slightly more than three-and-one-half centimeters in diameter. Most were *maru-bo,* or circular. The *hakaku-bo,* however, was hexagonal, and its angular edges made it viciously effective when unleashed against an unprotected target, since they cut along with the strike. Occasionally too, the length of the bo was inlaid or banded with strips of iron or other metal. This increased the strength of the bo considerably. Most techniques for countering the bo by the well-trained swordsman involved his using the katana to slash at the wooden bo at an angle that would hack through it, cutting the bo down and significantly reducing its effectiveness. With the protecting bands or strips of metal, the weapon was much more difficult to chop or cut and the bojutsu exponent was at a better advantage in the encounter.

Perhaps the short staff would have remained much as it was, a *fozoku bugei,* an auxillary weapon of the warrior's arsenal, never given the recognition of other, more finely crafted arms, had it not been for the burning ambition of a single man.

Gonnosuke's Shindo Muso-Ryu

Muso Gonnosuke Katsuyoshi was born in the 16th century in Japan. It was an age when the Shogun Tokugawa Ieyasu was in the process of unifying the entire nation under his domain, a time when feudal lords fought viciously among themselves, a time when the martial arts underwent a dramatic transformation that resulted in an unprecedented refinement of technique and training methods. Numerous ryu were founded, based mostly upon improving the concepts of more ancient schools, and others were more fully codified. It is not coincidence, considering the violence of the era and the opportunity for fighting, that a majority of Japan's martial arts masters lived during this period.

Both Katsuyoshi and Gonnosuke are popular names used by samurai families at that time, and so we can assume he was of samurai heritage. In addition, records state that Gonnosuke entered the Katori Shinto-ryu and later on, the Kashima Shinto-ryu. He was schooled in the full range of teachings of both these ryu. Had he not the familial background to permit him to train in the traditional warrior arts, he would not have been admitted to either ryu.

Gonnosuke took a special interest in the bojutsu of the Katori- and Kashima-ryu, excelling in the teachings of both styles. He then traveled to Edo (present-day Tokyo), where he entered into the customary rite of *musha-shugyo*. The word refers to the practice of visiting numerous dojo and masters of different schools, and requesting instruction or openly challenging. Musha-shugyo could be hazardous of course; even the best martial artist undergoing it would collect his share of injuries. But it was an excellent way to test one's skill and to learn as much as possible about the strategies of other styles of martial art.

Gonnosuke must have been extraordinarily able with the bo, for he met a number of exponents of assorted ryu and was not defeated in any matches. He also took the opportunity to train in several of their dojo, always refining his art. It was during this period of musha-shugyo that Gonnosuke met the swordsman Miyamoto Musashi.

There must be a dozen or more accounts of the climactic battles between Musashi and Muso Gonnosuke, most of them based upon little more than the vivid imaginations of fiction writers. Aside from the *kodan* (oral folktales), there is scant information about the duels. One source is the *Niten-Ki,* a biography of Musashi which mentions their initial encounter. The *Niten-Ki* is a collection of anecdotes told about Musashi by his followers and acquaintances. It was not compiled into book form until several years after Musashi's death. Its rendering of the conflict must therefore be taken with a grain of salt.

According to the *Niten-Ki,* the first match between Muso Gonnosuke and Musashi occurred while Musashi was staying near Kofu, just outside Edo proper. Musashi was sitting in a garden working on a bow he was making from a length of mulberry wood. Without warning, Gonnosuke approached and, dispensing with an introduction or even a bow, he shouted a challenge at Musashi, immediately swinging his bo in a potentially lethal attack. Without so much as rising from his seat, Musashi countered, avoiding the bo and striking Gonnosuke smartly with the unfinished piece of wood in his hand. The book records this incident as having taken place after Musashi's renowned battles with the Yoshioka family and before he became a retainer of the Hosokawa clan, which would place it *circa* 1610. Musashi would have been in his early 20s; Gonnosuke about the same age.

For the young warrior Gonnosuke, the ignominious defeat must have been crushing. He was not injured, save in his pride, but his belief in his skills with the bo doubtless had been shattered. Chagrined, he retreated to Kyushu, the southernmost island in the Japan archipelago which, during Gonnosuke's time, contained wild and uncivilized frontiers. Gonnosuke secreted himself at Homan-zan, a mountain in the northern part of Kyushu, surrounded by deep forests, smoking hot springs, and rock-strewn ravines and gorges. He filled his days with meditation and severely taxing practices with the bo, undergoing austere religious rituals as well. After a period of this monastic existence, Gonnosuke was visited with a dream.

Gonnosuke ascribed to his dream a divine manifestation. Such heavenly visions were far from unheard of in the martial arts of ancient Japan. A number of ryu had been founded, according to their scrolls and oral traditions, by masters who received enlightenment from the gods in the ways of combat. It is a phenomenon that goes as far back in history as the Minamoto general Yoshitsune, who was tutored in the craft of warfare by *tengu* (winged mountain sprites) who revealed principles of combat to the warlord when he was still a child. Usually, this sort of divine inspiration was commemorated when the master named his newly-born style, affixing *tenshin sho* or *tenshin shoden* to its title. The words indicate that the fundamentals of the art are the result of *tenshin*, a "divine presence."

The details of Gonnosuke's dream have been preserved, although anyone expecting enlightenment upon its revelation is apt to be disappointed. *"Maruki wo motte, suigetsu wo shirei"* (take a log and take control of the vital elements) is the way Gonnosuke himself described it.

Abstract as this divine command might be, it was the inspiration that encouraged Gonnosuke to re-evaluate his weapon. He promptly removed several centimeters of its length and began to take an entirely innovative approach to its use. This event marked the birth of the Shindo Muso-ryu, and the beginnings as well of the jo.

Gonnosuke referred to his art as Shindo Muso, or the Divine Way of Dream Thought. Training alone, he amassed a body of strategies with the shorter stick which were specifically designed to counter the strengths of the other weapons of the *bugeisha* (particularly the sword) and to exploit their weaknesses.

With this knowledge, Gonnosuke left his mountain hermitage in search of the man who had so easily beaten him. He did not have far to look, for Musashi had also come to the island of Kyushu, where he was employed in the service of Lord Hosokawa. Once again, Gonnosuke came to Musashi seeking a match. The two engaged in a furious fight. There is no way to be sure exactly what technique Gonnosuke used to defeat Musashi, but Musashi was thoroughly and convincingly beaten, for the only time in his life. Japan's most celebrated and colorful swordsman was bested by the art of the simple stick.

If Gonnosuke were a man of lesser quality, he would no doubt have advertised his victory and accumulated a fortune by teaching his art. The years of self-imposed exile, though, had changed his personality in some way. Once he'd proven the efficacy of his new art, he was content to retire quietly. He accepted a position as a teacher of martial arts with the Kuroda clan of Kyushu. To a select and very limited number of his students he revealed the art of his jo, but the Shindo Muso style remained a matter of *okuden* (secret teachings).

For several centuries, the secrets of jojutsu were handed down carefully and kept from the rest of the world. Along the way, a number of expert bugeisha who were initiated into its teachings added their own contributions, and the Shindo Muso style of the jo was augmented by methods from the Shinto-ryu of swordsmanship, as well as by ryu dealing with the sickle and chain, and techniques of binding an opponent with a short length of cord *(hojojutsu)*.

Other Schools

Further evolution of the jo however did not occur through the efforts of Shindo Muso-ryu alone. Martial scholars estimate that nearly 350 other classical bugei-ryu subsequently adopted various jo techniques in their schools. The methods of classical jojutsu, contained within the kata of these ryu, are incredibly diverse, dealing with every possible situation in which the practitioner might find himself. As with any traditional *ko-ryu,* most techniques with the jo features movements designed to counter an attack by a swordsman, the katana being the principal weapon of the feudal martial artist. But within these kata too, are a multitude of techniques to be used in confined spaces, against multiple opponents or when encumbered in armor.

Once Gonnosuke had proven the efficiency of the shorter staff in combat, his methods underwent experimentation and alteration. A substantial interest was shown by some bugeisha in further exploring the possibilities of this unpretentious weapon. They evolved a multitude of arts employing sticks of graduated sizes. Most notably, those which have survived into our century in a recognizable form include the *han-bo* and *tan-jo*. Both these staffs are shorter even than the jo and may be manipulated in ways to trap an opponent's attacking limb or weapon, bind him, or administer a collection of painful and incapacitating joint locks. Of course, they could also be used to strike or thrust, as with the longer jo. Because of their convenient length, they were adopted in various forms by police departments in Japan and used along with the jo in riot-control situations and other confrontations where firearms would be unnecessary or unwarranted. The selective means of transmitting the art of the jo however continued until early in the present century. Under the tutelage of Hanjiro Shirata, the 24th headmaster of Shindo Muso-ryu, a bugeisha named Takaji Shimizu began training in jojutsu in 1907. In 1914, he was granted a full *menkyo* (license) to teach. Shimizu, who was also an expert in a variety of other classical combative arts of Japan, researched the techniques of jojutsu extensively. In 1927, at the request of the National Police Agency in Tokyo, he and Ken'ichi Takayama, another master of the ryu, demonstrated jojutsu as a possible aid to law enforcement officers. Their methods were implemented, and Shimizu was appointed an instructor to a police unit specially selected to learn the art. This sub-specialty of jojutsu is referred to as *keijojutsu*—police stick art.

It was not until the 1950s that jojutsu was taught to members of the general public, and even then, qualifications for entrance to its dojo were strict and new students somewhat limited in number. In the early 60s, after much consideration and study, Takaji Shimizu decided to change the name of his art from jojutsu to jodo. The name reflected a number of alterations Shimizu had made in the art. He had eliminated from regular practice (but not from the curriculum entirely) a number of techniques that could have been dangerous to less-skilled practitioners. He instituted training in designated basic movements to further refine the teachings, and most importantly, he directed the art of the jo into a Way, a budo, meant not primarily as a means of combat but as a discipline by which to strive for self-perfection.

Today, the jo is practiced by exponents in nearly every corner of the world. It is a noble example of how the values of the classical budo, can benefit a modern society, retaining the strengths and profundity of another time.

Uyeshiba's Aiki-jo

The third major influence on the art of the jo came with the teachings of Morihei Uyeshiba, the founder of modern aikido. In many ways, Uyeshiba's aiki-jo is the most eclectic application of the short staff. It is also the most popularly taught form of the jo, practiced by thousands of aikidoka all over the world.

Uyeshiba was born in the 15th year of Meiji (1883), long enough ago that much of his martial arts education came under the instruction of bugeisha who'd had occasion to put their skills to practical effect. Sickly as a child, he soon developed a passionate interest in the classical martial arts. Throughout his early years, he apprenticed himself to a number of jujutsu and fencing masters, and trained as well in the arts of the spear and halberd.

A man with deep religious convictions, Uyeshiba eventually mingled the theologies of Buddhism and native Shinto to explain the strategy and philosophy of a new form of budo he created during the first part of the 20th century. Along with an explanation of the rationale of his budo, which was a morality based upon mysticism, he included an approach to combat (or to avoiding it) which stressed a physical and mental center that could be directed to control oneself or others. His aikido was essentially circular in nature, not, it is important to note, in the sense of evading an attack, as is commonly thought, but rather in the sense of entering directly against it and countering with any of several circular projections.

One of the outstanding characteristics of Uyeshiba's combative philosophy was that the principles of his aikido were universal truths. They could be applied to physical self-defense as well as in dealing with others to create a more harmonious society. Likewise, he reasoned that a neutralization of a single opponent was no different than that of overcoming a dozen enemies. Too, Uyeshiba maintained that those techniques which could be executed empty handed could also be performed with a weapon in one's possession. The principles of movement from the hips, centering one's strength, and so on, were exactly the same with a sword or a staff, or without either. To improve the skills of his disciples, Uyeshiba demanded rigorous practice with the wooden sword, or *bokken*, and exercises with the jo.

Aiki-jo, as Uyeshiba Sensei's method may be called, is an eclectic form. Like the exercises he introduced with the bokken, they do not belong specifically to any single ryu. The techniques of the jo which are taught in most aikido dojo are an amalgamation, not intended to represent any style or preserve a single combative tradition, but to illustrate the principles of aikido as they may be applied with a polearm. Too, the student is schooled to regard the jo as an extension of his arms and body, and so he treats it not as a separate entity, but as an extension of the normal motion of his body. There is scarcely a single precept of aikido which cannot be demonstrated with the jo and through its implementation many ideas can be more adequately expressed or studied. It was a maxim of Uyeshiba's that when an aikidoka was having difficulty with his *taijutsu* (empty-handed forms), he should turn to the use of the bokken or the jo to gain a different perspective.

The founder of aikido called upon his expertise in *sojutsu* (spear art) to formulate his aiki-jo, but he insisted that the actual length or particular type of polearm was not important. For this reason, there are photographs of him performing the same techniques he taught with the regular jo, wielding a spear, or a spike-like pole used in hunting wild boar, and with staffs of differing lengths. For Uyeshiba's aikido, the principles of movement and the stability of the center were what mattered.

Today, in the jodo of Shindo Muso-ryu, in the jojutsu of the various koryu in Japan, and in Uyeshiba's aiki-jo, the art of the jo is maintained and nurtured. It has survived considerable and far-reaching social changes in Japan and has even been exported to other countries. As well, it is the only weapon that has survived to be practiced, without alteration in its forms or appearance, in all three versions of the martial arts and Ways: classical bojutsu, classical budo, and the modern or *shin* budo. Not, upon reflection, an unworthy accomplishment for an ordinary stick of wood.

EQUIPMENT AND PREPARATIONS FOR TRAINING

If a certain kind of beauty may be considered to have reached its zenith in simplicity, then the jo might easily qualify as one of the most beautiful weapons of old Japan. Further, it is an implement that takes on a patina and a polished appearance with time. Jo, which have endured daily training and have been handled and burnished in practice, gradually exude an inner glow, as if animated by the spirit of the wielder. Such a weapon really does become an extension of the user's body, as well as a visible expression of the state of his soul. It must, therefore, be treated not as an "ordinary pole," but as a valued possession.

Types of Wood

Although a jo will infrequently crack or splinter, especially when struck against a bokken or another jo in training, a good one will last for many, many years. Selecting or constructing one then, should be a careful process.

Traditionally, jo are made of either white or red oak. Both grow abundantly in Japan and their heartwoods produce a long straight grain with just enough flexibility to overcome any brittleness when they have been dried and cured. Heartwood is lumber taken from that part of the tree nearest the core of the trunk. It is in this area that the grain of the wood tends to be the densest. Generally speaking, if one holds two jo made of the same wood and the same size, the heavier of the two will be the one carved of heartwood.

In a martial arts supply store, the prospective jo student may also find jo made of other woods, like loquat *(biwa),* or *sunuke.* Each of these will have advantages and disadvantages in terms of strength, grain, and weight. Price too, will be a factor in selection, for some woods like sunuke or ebony are rare and difficult to work with, making them expensive. Equally as interesting and probably cheaper is the challenge of making one's own jo. Later, the trainee may experiment, turning out jo of woods like ash, persimmon, and ironwood (hornbeam). Any of these will finish beautifully and the handmade jo will more than repay the time spent in the project.

Selecting a Jo

On obtaining a good jo, the student should examine first the grain. It must be running straight and longitudinally down the jo. It should be free of any knots or other blemishes that threaten to weaken it.

Hold the jo, or the piece of wood you intend to carve against your solar plexus, leaning forward slightly so the distant end rests against the floor. Reaching down now, you should be able to grip it close to its center and, by pulling towards you, you should feel the wood give a bit. It will not flex like a bow of course, but there should be just a little play, which will insure the correct flexibility.

The jo's weight is also important. There may be exemptions, but for most exponents, it is desirable to find as heavy a jo as possible. This facilitates training, strengthening the body and encouraging the essential contractions and expansions of the muscles necessary to control the weapon accurately when it is in motion. There are jo almost feather light, which can be whipped about with impressive speed, but the practitioner using one of these has no opportunity to get the feel of the real thing or to handle it correctly. Jo of acceptable weight range from approximately one to two pounds.

Clearly, a central consideration in the selection of a jo is in the trueness of its lines. A warp can demonstrably affect the jo's balance. It is difficult to find wood which has been treated and cured properly so it will resist warping. Hurrying along their products, many wood shops and lumberyards sell wood which was hastily treated with chemicals to get it to dry, or which is marketed while still green. All too quickly, this wood will bend and warp. Often, warping is not entirely the fault of the wood itself. In some parts of the country a high humidity acts on a jo, causing a warp even if the wood is solid and well treated.

Care of the Jo

We cannot change the weather, but there are some preventative steps that may be taken to reduce or eliminate serious warping. Jo should never be leaned against a wall or rested anywhere but on a perfectly flat surface. Stacking them in a corner is a sure way to induce warping and this can occur under the right circumstances, overnight. If a suitable *kake* (weapons rack) is unavailable, this may necessitate storing the jo directly on the floor. Lacking floor space, a workable alternative is to hang the jo suspended in a closet. To do this, bore a tiny hole in one end of the jo, just deep enough to screw in a small metal eyelet of the sort used to attach a picture frame to the hanging wire. A cord or another hook can be clipped through the eyelet to hang the jo vertically. When it is used, simply unscrew the eyelet and take the jo down.

After training, especially if it has been conducted outdoors in rainy weather, make sure the jo is dry before storing it away, since moisture will contribute to warping.

To test for a warp, lay the jo on a flat hard floor and roll it gently. If its lines are straight, it will roll across the floor with a minimum of noise. A bumping, clattering roll is an obvious sign of warpage.

Aside from the precautions to prevent warping, keeping the jo dry and never leaned against anything, it will need very little care. The practitioner might find that an occasional application of tung or linseed oil will help maintain the smoothness of the finish, and when carrying the jo to and from training, it should be stored in a cloth *fukuro*, a long bag that can be tied shut at the end, to protect the weapon. It should not even need be stated that any application of colorful paint or other such decoration immediately puts the practitioner into the category of circus performer rather than that of a serious budoka.

Dimensions of the Jo

The reader may wonder why what would seem to be a crucial matter, has not been addressed; that being the length of the jo. In jodo and jojutsu the exact length of the weapon is fixed according to the dictates of the ryu. Approximately 128 centimeters (about two-and-one-half centimeters in circumference) is standard for most ryu. The measurements of the jo in these schools was not a matter of guesswork or convenience, but carefully figured and codified for several reasons. The student of aiki-jo though, may use whatever length of jo he finds most suitable. Better yet, he should follow the advice of his teacher or his seniors. Many students prefer to keep two or three of differing measurements, training in turn with each of them. The jo used for the illustrations in this book are 128 and 127 centimeters. But I have practiced the same techniques using jo up to 138 centimeters. Perhaps the best standard of jo measurement should be this: the jo should reach at least to the level of the practitioner's solar plexus when stood vertically in front of him. It should not exceed 153 centimeters, a length which brings it into the category of a bo. In case the reader is wondering as to the distinction between the two; that is it. As a general rule of thumb, those staffs under five feet are considered jo; those over that are bo.

Proper Attire

Although training with the jo may be done in any comfortable, loose-fitting clothes, proper attire goes a long way in establishing a correct spirit and attitude about the art. Like aikido, the jo is customarily practiced in a heavy cotton jacket called a *uwagi,* similar to the kind worn in judo and white in color. While students may see black or dark blue cotton uwagi, there are some reasons to avoid wearing it. Usually, it identifies someone training in a classical budo. The earnest student of aiki-jo or of any other modern budo would not wish to seem to be presenting himself as something he's not, and will therefore shy away from this color in his training jacket.

The *joba hakama,* the wide, split-legged and pleated skirt of the samurai, is worn over a light pair of pants *(zubon)* for jo practice. The hakama tends to flare out and move around, accentuating the leg and hip motions of the wearer and for this very practical reason, it is a good idea to use it, to check to see if the movements are being done with the proper actions. A wide *obi* (sash) is wrapped several times around the waist underneath the hakama to keep the jacket closed. Its color should be plain, black or white, but it signifies nothing beyond its utilitarian function.

The uwagi and zubon underneath the hakama will absorb a lot of perspiration and should be aired between every training session and washed frequently. The hakama must be aired as well and folded properly to keep its creases and pleats. Although it will soon—with heavy training—be necessary to patch and mend the uniform, the wearer's abilities will in no way be enhanced by the application of gaudy insignia. These are completely antithetical to the spirit of the budo and they have no place in serious training. The true budoka appreciates a quiet, well-worn simplicity and has no need to attract attention to himself by affecting garish or pretentious costume.

Where to Train

Finally, the practitioner of the jo will need to consider a place to train. Ideally, some of his training will take place in a dojo, a "place for following the Way," with a smooth, raised wooden floor and an absence of decoration or other distractions. However, the student should make every effort to train outdoors in a variety of weather conditions and settings. This latter should not be construed as advice to go off swinging the jo in the halls of the nearest shopping mall or to show off on the front lawn. When training outside, try to find a peacefully rural or park-like area where there is a minimum of disturbances and onlookers. This preference for seclusion and privacy in the engagement of a serious and meaningful activity is, like the budoka's preference for a simple and unadorned training weapon and uniform, a sign of his style and commitment.

KIHON
(FUNDAMENTALS)

Knowledge of a wide range of techniques is entirely superfluous unless you thoroughly understand the fundamentals *(kihon)* of this art. While the kihon may take up only a small portion of this text, they are unquestionably its crux. If they are perfected and polished and completely grasped, the more advanced movements and techniques will be assimilated at a remarkably easier pace. Rushing on to higher-level methods by skimping on a severe practice of the basics cannot but result in frustration and failure.

Study carefully the instructions for holding the jo and make an effort to discern the way they complement movements of the body in these kihon. Pay particular attention to the stances *(kamae)*. They are the result of centuries of experimentation, frequently conducted on the ultimate testing ground—the battlefield. The way we hold the jo in a particular posture is the most effective way of holding it, *period.* Those masters who created these kamae did so at the risk of their lives and until or unless you have done the same sort of experimenting, stick with the traditional methods.

Finally, a technical note: for the purposes of clarification, the end of the jo nearest the body in these illustrations is called the near end. The tip farther away from the body (which will also usually be the striking end) is called the far end.

There are three basic ways to grip the jo; with its length protruding from the top of the fists, with it extending from the bottom of the fist, and a combination of the two. These are referred to respectively as *honte nigiri, gyakute nigiri,* and *ketsugo nigiri.*

The wrists should be firm but relaxed and the elbows should be bent just slightly, acting as shock absorbers. Gripping the jo too rigidly, or with arms and wrists stiffened, will reduce flexibility and speed and can result in injury. Held properly, the jo appears to be almost an extension of the arms and a natural part of the body.

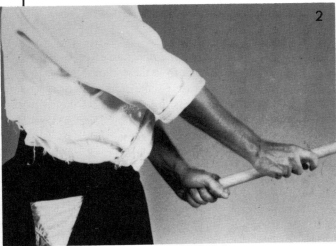

Honte Nigiri
(Basic Grip)

To seize the jo in honte nigiri, grip first with the left hand, taking the jo so the little finger is curled around directly beneath the jo's butt, *(kontei)*. The ring finger should be squeezed firmly around the last inch of the jo's shaft, with the middle and forefingers holding securely but not rigidly. The right hand is applied in the same way, little and ring fingers holding most firmly. The right forefinger should be held loosely enough on the jo's shaft so it points forward slightly. There should be the span of about two fist-widths between the grip of right and left hands. In thrusting motions the grip may be widened, but otherwise remains the same.

Gyakute Nigiri
(Reverse Grip)

Gyakute nigiri requires the jo to be held with the hands turned over, protruding from the bottom or little finger part of the fist. Until the wrists become more flexible, many beginning students may have to consciously relax the middle, ring, and little fingers on the leading hand in order to thrust with the jo in this grip.

Ketsugo Nigiri
(Combination Hand Grip)

Some techniques may be performed with the hands in a combination of the first two gripping methods, which is known as ketsugo nigiri. In this case, the far hand is in gyakute nigiri, the close hand is held in honte nigiri.

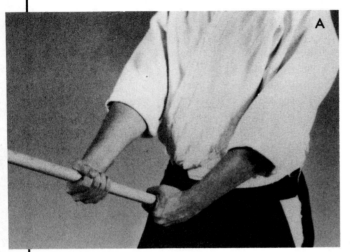

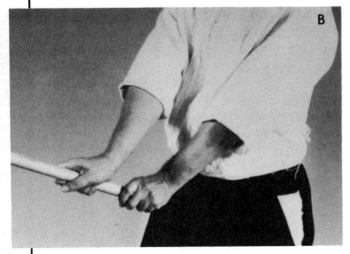

Incorrect Grips

Incorrect methods of holding the jo include: (A) hands twisted out too far, or (B) in too much; (C) held too closely together, or (D) on the wrong part of the jo. In gyakute nigiri, avoid (E) twisting

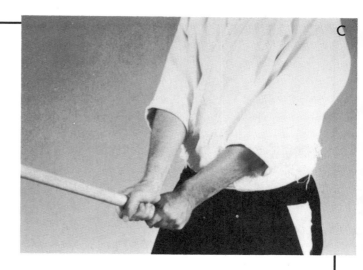

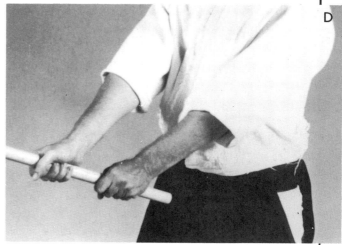

the wrists and arms unnaturally. In every grip, be aware that should the jo be forcefully connected with a target, the thumbs do not receive the concussive shock of the blow.

FRONT VIEW

SIDE VIEW

Sankakudai
(Triangular Stance)

The basic posture for jo training is *sankakudai,* the "triangular stance," which is also known as *hanmi* (half-facing). It affords rapid and controlled movement in almost every direction and maintains a solid stability. All basic kamae in jo training are performed beginning in sankakudai. To assume it, position the feet slightly wider than shoulder width. The rear foot is turned out at approximately a 45-degree angle, with the front foot pointed straight ahead. Body weight should be centered evenly, with hip and buttock muscles taut. The toes of both feet should be tensed, as if gripping the floor, and there should be just enough space between the heels and the floor to slide the thickness of a sheet of paper in between. The most common error in assuming sankakudai is to turn the rear foot out at too great an angle, resembling something like the back stance *(kokutsu dachi)* of karate-do. This is fundamentally incorrect and greatly inhibits movement to the sides and rear when using the jo.

Chudan Kamae
(Middle Level Posture)

The elementary kamae of jo training is the *chudan kamae* (middle level posture). The jo's near end is about a fist's width from the abdomen, with the far end projecting directly at the level where an opponent's throat would be. Your weight is evenly distributed on both feet in sankakudai.

LEFT CHUDAN KAMAE

RIGHT CHUDAN KAMAE

FRONT VIEW

Jodan Kamae
(Upper Level Posture)

In *jodan kamae* (upper level posture) the jo is held in a nearly horizontal position above the head. Take care not to hold the butt of the jo too high, keeping it instead nearly level with the forehead. Proper jodan kamae demands the elbows be bent, providing a springy support as well as protection for the head. Although the hips should be turned fully to the front in jodan, the upper body is twisted marginally to keep the jo in a direct midline with the torso.

SIDE VIEW

FRONT VIEW

Waki Kamae
(Rear Angle Posture)

Two other stances commonly seen in jo pracitce are the right *(migi)* and left *(hidare) waki kamae.* The jo is held in honte nigiri and pointed down and back at your side. The jo is positioned on a line parallel with the back foot. It is important to extend the rear arm naturally and hold the opposite hand directly in front of the abdomen.

SIDE VIEW

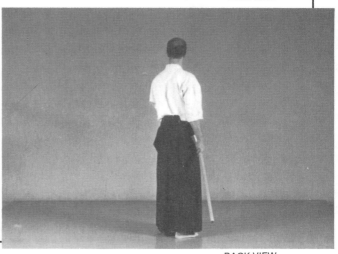

BACK VIEW

1

2

Walking and Sitting

Before proceeding with the methods of using the jo, it would be pertinent to demonstrate an example of *sa-ho* (etiquette). When walking about the training area but not actually practicing, (1)

carry the jo against your side, pointing down. To be seated, (2-4) pass the jo around to the left side. (5&6) Bend down without bending over, and adjust the inner folds of your hakama with

Continued

6

your right hand. (7) Drop to your left knee, slanting the jo to your front. (8) Adjust the right hem of your haka-ma if necessary, and (9) place the jo on your left side.

7

If necessary, adjust the left hem of the hakama with your left hand. (10) Move first your right, then your left hand atop your thighs and sit squarely and straight.

UCHI KATA
(STRIKING METHODS)

The jo may be used in striking actions in almost exactly the same way the sword is used to cut. Therefore, it is possible to strike with the jo in the six basic methods of cutting with the sword: straight overhead *(shomen uchi),* left and right diagonal *(hidari* and *migi naname),* left and right side *(hidari* and *migi yoko uchi),* and the thrust *(tsuki).* In addition, the jo can be used to sweep *(barai)* or strike from angles of attack that go from low to high or high to low, largely because of the freedom you have in lengthening, shortening, or reversing your grip on the weapon. This chapter covers the more elementary of these, concentrating on those which occur most predominantly in formal exercises with the jo.

Since much of the play and games of childhood involve swinging a stick of one kind or another, it's natural to suppose such actions are relatively simple and require little practice. When attempting to focus a blow at exactly the spot intended though, to do it well, exposing as few defensive gaps as possible, and utilizing all the body's power, even the most ordinary strikes can become quite difficult. Given daily training, the basic methods of striking explained here cannot be done with even a minimum of proficiency by the beginner without more than a year's practice. For that reason, limit early efforts to performing the action exactly right, without attempting to develop power or speed until the movements are natural.

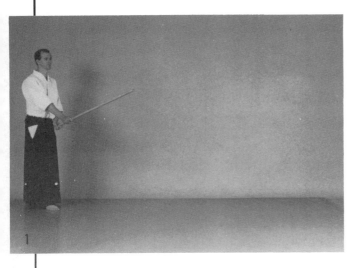

Shomen Uchi
(Front Strike)

(1) Beginning in a right chudan kamae (2) step straight forward with your left leg, raising the jo to jodan level, and turning your right foot out to a 45-degree angle. (3) Strike down in such a way that the jo retraces precisely the same vertical arc in which it was raised. The step forward is finished at the same instant the jo is focused at the completion of the strike, which should end at the chudan level. (4) Continue moving forward, stepping forward with your right foot and turning your left out 45 degrees as you raise the jo to jodan

level. (5) Strike down vertically, focusing your blow at chudan level as you simultaneously complete your step forward. Shomen uchi should be executed so the feet always return to the sankakudai stance in which the movement was begun. Take care not to bring them closer together, or leave them farther apart as you move. Also remember to maintain the correct jodan posture when the jo is raised above the head. Once this movement feels comfortable, shomen uchi should also be practiced moving to the rear.

Naname Uchi
(Diagonal Strike)

When the jo's striking path is at an angle approximately 45 degrees from vertical, the blow is referred to as naname uchi. (Often, especially in aikido dojo, this angle of attack is called *yoko uchi* (side strike). To distinguish it from a more laterally directed uchi of that same name, however, we use the term *naname,* meaning "at an angle.") The target of naname uchi may be the temple, the neck, or the shoulder. In training, it should follow at the angle as if one were striking down on a line following the outer lapel of the *keikogi* jacket. To execute naname uchi, (1) begin in a right chudan kamae. (2) Cant the jo off to the side as you (3) raise it above your head, (4&5) swinging it around in an ellipsis and (6) striking down smoothly as you complete the step forward. Repeat the process for the other side, (7) cant

Continued

the jo off to the left side as you (8) raise it overhead, stepping forward with your right foot. (9) Continue to swing it around in an ellipsis, and (10) strike down diagonally as you complete your step forward. (11) Continue to move forward as you again cant the jo off to the right side, (12) raising it above your head and stepping forward with your left foot. (13) Continue to swing it around in an ellipsis, and (14) strike down diagonally as you complete your step forward. Naname uchi may be performed moving to the rear as well, focusing the blow at the same time the rear foot touches down.

Gedan Barai
(Lower Level Sweep)

While the name of this technique, *gedan barai,* implies a swinging, reaping action, it may also be employed as a kind of *barai uchi,* a sweeping strike. It is illustrative of the many and diverse ways in which the jo may be wielded. (1) Beginning in chudan kamae to the right, (2) slide the jo to the rear with the left hand, keeping the right still but allowing the jo to slide through. When the far end of the jo touches the right hand grip, (3) begin to step forward, lowering the jo. (4) Swinging it up in a scoop-like movement, (5) coincide the focus of the strike with the completion of the body's forward movement. Then (6) draw the jo back again, this time with the right hand and (7&8) repeat the strike from the opposite side of the body. When performing gedan barai, pay particular attention that the body rotates at the same time the jo is brought forward.

Age Uchi
(Rising Strike)

Age uchi demonstrates another way in which the jo may be swung to strike from the oblique angle. (1) Assume the left waki kamae position. (2&3) Commencing a step to the front, swing the jo down and out at a right angle to the body. (4) As the step is completed, raise the jo and at the same time lower the body into a slight crouch to give impetus to the upward strike. (5) Draw the jo back again, this time with the right, rear hand, and (6&7) repeat the strike on the opposite side of the body. It is important to "sink" the hips and to keep the arms no higher than head level to attain maximum speed and correct application of power in age uchi. Age uchi may also be executed by lifting the lead hand above the head before the strike is begun, as demonstrated in the section on combinations.

5

Age uchi and naname uchi, done from a *handachi* (kneeling) position, are but two examples of the way power may be increased by lowering the body dramatically at the moment of impact. These techniques occur frequently in the *tandoku renshu* that follows in this book. However, it must be remembered that in striking from such a low posture, further rapid movement may be difficult and you risk putting yourself into a dangerously disadvantageous position. You should practice these basic forms severely, strengthening hips and legs, to allow you to drop rapidly and immediately rise again upon completion of the strike.

Naname Uchi Handachi (Diagonal Strike to Kneeling Position)

This is an angle strike from kneeling, another version of naname uchi which may be performed as a sweeping barai by dropping into a crouch as the strike is deliv-

ered. (1) Begin in right chudan kamae, and (2) step forward. (3) Swing the jo to the rear, then (4&5) in the same motion raise it above your

 Continued

head. (6&7) Continue by striking down on a 45-degree diagonal as if executing naname uchi. However, (8&9) instead of focusing the blow at chudan level, continue swinging down, dropping into a crouch, and (10&11) slash broadly with the jo in a wide arc that ends as the crouch is set. The jo

must finish its sweeping arc well behind (to the rear) of the body. However, it must be held and controlled in a position to be able to strike again quickly. Naname uchi handachi may also be done from a left chudan kamae, with the left hand leading on the jo.

1

2

Age Uchi Handachi (Rising Strike to Kneeling Position)

Age uchi can be performed from a kneeling crouch as well. (1) Starting from a right chudan position, (2) begin the strike as you would a basic age uchi, pulling the jo back with the left hand while the right hand remains still but allows the jo to slide through. (3) As the far end of the jo comes into the right hand, (4) begin to drop the body in a low crouch that is completed at the same time the jo focuses. It is important here upon focus of the strike to keep the striking end of the jo at a level below the top of the head.

3

4

The most common errors in performing *tsuki* are found in the grip. If either hand is too tight on the jo, the weapon is unable to slide freely and quickly. If the hands are too loose, especially the hand nearest the target, there is no way a proper trajectory will be accomplished. Using the leading hand merely as a guide to aim the blow may deliver the butt of the jo to the target, but the blow will be poorly focused, easily parried, and unlikely to inflict any damage. Even if the fingers are relaxed, the jo must fit snugly in the palm of the leading hand and be gripped firmly at the instant of focus.

Honte Tsuki
(Basic Hand Thrust)

There are a number of ways of performing the straight thrust *(honte tsuki)* with the jo. An excellent way to learn and practice it calls for (1) starting in a left chudan kamae. With the right hand, (2) slide the jo to the rear, leaving the left hand stationary but allowing the jo to slide through. At the same time, (3) begin a step forward with the right foot. As the right foot passes the left, swing the jo around to the left side of the body and pull it back so it is parallel with the hips. The hands

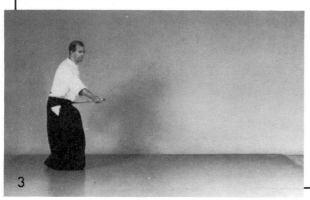

should be grasping the jo at both ends. (4) Continue the step forward, maintaining a firm grip on the jo with the left hand, sliding it through the right fist, until the moment of focus. The tsuki (thrust) should be focused at exactly the same time the jo slides into the normal grip space. Continue with the exercise, (5) pulling back with the left hand, (6) swinging the jo around to the right side of the body, pulling it back to a position parallel with the hips and (7) thrusting again.

Gyakute Tsuki
(Reverse Thrust)

The *tsuki* (thrust with the jo) may also be made with the jo in the reverse hand grip, and this is referred to as *gyakute* (reverse tsuki). (1) Proceeding from a right chudan kamae, (2) lift the jo straight up with the right hand, leaving the left hand as it is. (3) Rotate the jo around in a wide arc and as it comes down to just below shoulder level, (4) thrust it forward, gliding the jo through the left fist. The left hand is relaxed, gripping the jo principally with the fore and middle finger and thumb. Continue the movement, (5) retracting the jo fully, (6&7) twisting the body and stepping forward at the same time, to (8) thrust from the opposite side.

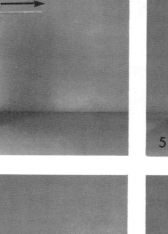

Ushiro Tsuki
(Rear Thrust)

To perform ushiro tsuki, (1) assume once again, right chudan kamae. Push the jo forward, as if making a thrust, then (2) pull the jo with the left hand to the side of the left hip. At the same time, begin lowering yourself and reach out, sliding the right hand all the way to the far end of the jo. (3) Step back, turning your head to look over your left shoulder to make visual contact with the target, and (4) thrust the jo to the rear through the right fist. The jo's thrust should be completed as the step is finished. Note that at the completion of ushiro tsuki, the right hand is pressed firmly against the abdomen; the left arm is bent enough to keep the jo at the correct, middle level. It is especially important that the head be turned and the target be in sight before the thrust is fully launched. Failure to do so when working with a real opponent can result in injury, and unless the practitioner is fully aware of the path and trajectory of his weapon, he cannot be said to have total control over it or himself.

71

RENWAKU WAZA
(COMBINATION TECHNIQUES)

It is reasonable enough to assume that the function of *renwaku waza* (combination techniques) is (or *was,* in ancient times) to increase the possibilities available to the exponent in combat, rendering him more effective in an encounter. If he had ten techniques at his disposal, it might be supposed, he'd be twice as effective as a warrior equipped with only five. To some extent there is validity in this supposition. Certainly someone who relies on a single attack is going to find himself in serious trouble if his opponent has a good counter for it. On the other hand, it is a mistake to assume the practitioner with the largest or most varied arsenal will be superior in every encounter. In classical combat, the warrior was educated to consider every *waza* (technique) complete unto itself, sufficient to accomplish his purposes. Naturally, he practiced multiple techniques or renwaku waza but he treated each of them in the sequence as lethal. Today, we may often find budoka who hurry through combinations with the idea in mind of employing the first merely as a hastily offered feint. Others may seek to impress onlookers by flashing through a series of strikes with dazzling speed, none of them focused or controlled. Neither approach has a place in the practice of renwaku waza. It must be assumed, even in the dojo where training is theoretical, that there will be no second chance. The initial action must be delivered with complete resolve. It should never be blended in with a succeeding waza.

Combination techniques encourage nimble movement and promote an improvement in overall skills. Because of the great versatility of the jo, they are nearly endless in number and with practice the exponent should be able to link together any number of the kihon in varying order, making all of them in a steady and effective flow. Included here are a few examples. Please keep in mind that the renwaku waza, properly performed, will not look like a series or a step-by-step sequence, but a single, controlled technique.

Shomen Uchi/Tsuki
(Front Strike and Thrust)

(1) Begin in a right chudan kamae. (2&3) Step forward, striking with shomen uchi as the left foot advances. (4) Pause at the focus of the blow, slightly lowering the body. (5) Extend the right hand to the distal tip of the jo. (6&7) Slide the left foot to the rear, at the same time thrusting the jo in that direction. Be certain to look back over your shoulder at this moment. Complete the tsuki at the same time the rearward step finishes. This combination may be done from the left chudan kamae as well, reversing the action.

Age Uchi/Shomen Uchi (Rising Strike and Front Strike)

(1) Take a right chudan position. (2) Raise the right hand and the jo with it until the weapon is nearly vertical and slightly to the left side of the body. (3) Step forward and strike upward with age

uchi. Pause at the instant of focus then, (4) leaving the left hand as it is, draw the jo to the rear with the right hand. (5) Step forward and (6) strike with shomen uchi.

Gedan Barai/Naname Uchi (Lower Level Sweep and Diagonal Strike)

(1) Begin in a left waki kamae. (2) Step forward with the left foot and strike at the gedan level with a barai stroke of the jo. (3) Keeping the left hand as it is, slide the jo to the rear with the right hand. (4) Grip the jo firmly with the left hand and

(5) step forward with the right foot, sliding the right hand down the jo. (6) Strike at the correct angle for naname uchi. The same combination may be performed beginning from a right waki kamae.

Happo Uchi
(Eight Directions Striking)

Happo uchi means literally eight directions striking. Like *happo giri* of swordsmanship, it is a fundamental exercise with considerable and far-reaching benefits. Fundamentally, happo uchi instructs in the process of encountering mutliple opponents. The series of shifting and simultaneously executing attacks is a cornerstone of all Japanese budo, demonstrating the maxim of *kobo ichi:* attack and defense as one. Properly coordinated breathing during happo uchi teaches rhythm and timing and allows maximization of power through body, weapon, and spirit in a single devastating moment. This is referred to as *ichibyoshi uichi:* striking in a single, unified instant. Happo uchi also instills a mental state of concentration that allows each attack to be performed with 100-percent effort and then immediately withdrawn as the next one begins. When faced with a number of opponents, each must be dealt with separately and yet paradoxically, they must all be treated as one, a single unit. To commence happo uchi, (1) assume a right chudan kamae. (2&3) Without changing stances or body position, strike with shomen uchi. (4) Keeping the right leg forward, slide forward half a pace and thrust. (5&6) Pivot 180 degrees to your left, and (7) strike again with shomen uchi. This sequence is a strike, followed by a thrust and then another overhead strike in the opposite direction. But all these must flow together in a continuous action. It may help to imagine two opponents threatening from front and rear. As you strike with the initial shomen uchi, the front opponent steps back to avoid it. Still he prepares another assault and the rear opponent begins to attack as well. You must thrust against the front opponent and at the same time slide away from the rear opponent's move, turning, and countering. After having struck the rear opponent with shomen uchi, (8) slide forward

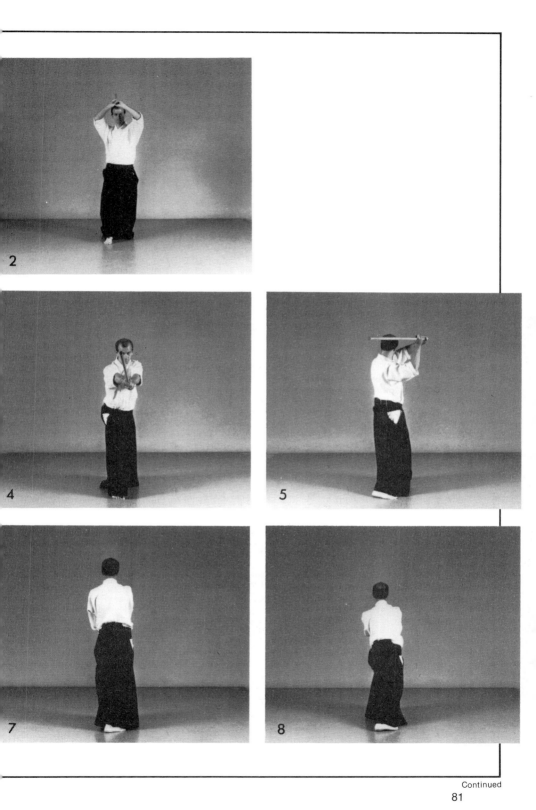

2

4

5

7

8

Continued

again and execute another tsuki. (9-11) Pivot to your right 270 degrees, (12) striking down again with shomen uchi. (13) Sliding forward about half a pace, thrust in that direction and (14&15) immediately pivot 180 degrees around to your right and (16) strike with shomen uchi. (17) Ex-

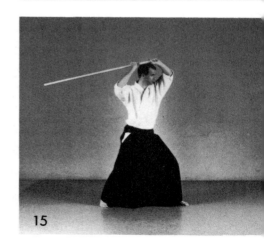

10 11

13 14

16 17

Continued

ecute tsuki in that direction. (18-21) Pivot to your right 315 degrees by drawing the rear right foot up until it touches the left or nearly so. The right leg is the *jiku ashi* (pivot leg) upon which your weight is borne. When you have completed the spin, (22) shift your weight to the left side and step out with the right foot to execute the shomen uchi. Once again, slide up half a step and (23) thrust. (24& 25) Pivot quickly to your left 180 degrees and (26&27) strike with shomen uchi.

19

20

22

23

25

26

Continued

(28) Slide and thrust. (29) Pivot 270 degrees to your right, (30) turning around and (31) striking with shomen uchi. (32) Thrust in this same direction, sliding forward, then (33) pivot 180 degrees to your left and (34&35) strike with a final shomen uchi. You are now, at the conclusion of happo uchi, facing to the right rear corner of where you began.

28

29

31

32

34

35

TANDOKU RENSHU
(FORMAL SOLO EXERCISE)

The following is a formal exercise with the jo—not a kata—but what is called a *tandoku renshu*. The name refers to a solo practice. It is without some of the subtlety and profundity of a true kata yet the tandoku exercise is in its own right a training method of significant worth. It combines the basics of the jo with a wide variety of body movement, shifting, and changing directions. It demands balance and power and speed. It tests all the skills of the practitioner, revealing his weaknesses unerringly and providing a constant standard by which he may measure his progress.

Learning the details of rhythm and timing in an exercise like this is best accomplished when a qualified teacher is physically present to demonstrate and correct. This text therefore, is intended to serve more as a reference and a guide.

The directions given for performing the tandoku renshu indicate the most obvious meaning behind them. The section on bunkai however demonstrates a greater depth of meaning and implementation against an opponent.

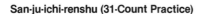

San-ju-ichi-renshu (31-Count Practice)

Movement 1

(1a) Begin in a left sankakudai stance. Place the jo perpendicularly at your left front corner. Grip the jo with your left hand so that fist is at the chudan level. The right hand is at your side. Your weight should be extended forward a bit. (1b) Seize the jo with your right hand in ketsugo nigiri. (1c&1d) Use the left hand as a fulcrum, pushing the far end of the jo out in a circle, and

(1e&1f) back. This movement resembles the J-stroke a canoeist makes with his paddle. (1g) With body and stance remaining as they are, (1h&1i) draw the jo around to your right side. (1j) Slide the front foot forward, and execute tsuki. The left hand rotates over during the thrust.

Continued

Movement 2

Without changing the grip on the jo, (2a&2b) slide your left foot back and to the right side, drawing the jo up and over your head. The far jo tip should be just below your own chudan level. Twist your hips sharply to the right. Although the left foot is retracted dramatically, it is important to keep the body center stationary.

2 a

3 a

3 b

Movement 4

(4a-4c) Execute *jodan gaeshi* (upper level reversal) by raising the jo overhead and rotating it

4 a

Movement 3

(3a&3b) Pull the left foot in toward your right foot, then (3c&3d) slide it to your front, simultaneously executing another honte tsuki.

2 b

3 c

3 d

4 b

4 c

Continued

clockwise with your right hand. (4d) Switch grips with your left hand by moving it forward to the end of the jo. Then (4e) step forward with your right foot to strike the first of four *renzoku* (successive) naname uchi. Pay attention to the movement of both hands during the reversal.

4 d

5 a

5 b

5 e

Movement 6

Without changing the relative position of your left, (6a-6c) pivot 180 degrees to your right on

4e

Movement 5

(5a-5c) Step forward again and (5d&5e) strike with naname uchi. You should be striking at an angle from high left to low right.

5c

5d

5a

6b

Continued

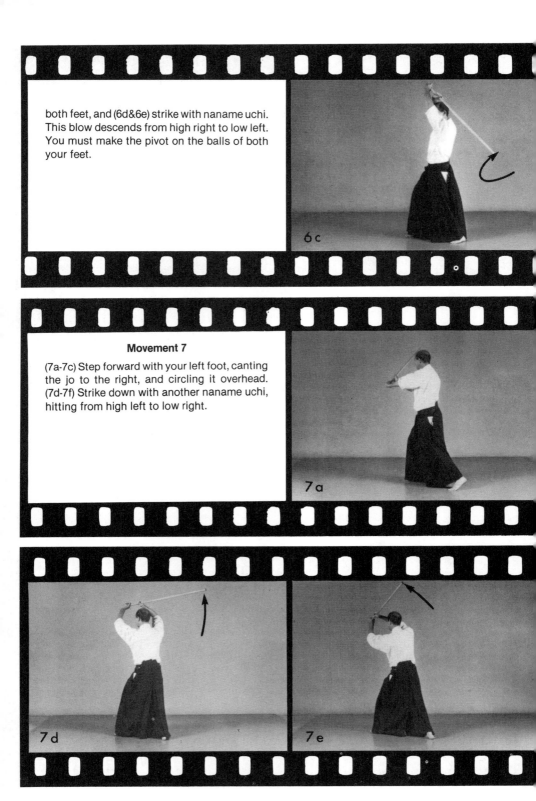

both feet, and (6d&6e) strike with naname uchi. This blow descends from high right to low left. You must make the pivot on the balls of both your feet.

6 c

Movement 7

(7a-7c) Step forward with your left foot, canting the jo to the right, and circling it overhead. (7d-7f) Strike down with another naname uchi, hitting from high left to low right.

7 a

7 d

7 e

96

Movement 8

(8a-8c) Pivot completely around to your right on the balls of both feet. Pivot a bit more than 180 degrees, executing *yoko barai ushi* (side sweep strike) by swinging the jo in a broad horizontal arc at chudan level, then (8d&8e) follow through by stepping back with your right foot.

8 a

8 d

8 e

9 b

9 c

b

8c

Movement 9

(9a-9d) Strike upward with age uchi, stepping forward with your right foot. This strike follows a narrow angle from your right rear corner. Do not pause at all between movements 8 and 9.

9 a

d

Movement 10

(10a) Cant the jo to the right, circling it over-head, and then (10b) step forward with your left foot, (10c&10d) simultaneously striking down with shomen uchi.

10 a

10 d

Movement 11

(11a-11b) Reach out with your left hand, slidin it up to the far end of the jo. (11c) As your le hand seizes the jo's tip, (11d) execute geda honte tsuki by lowering the tip and thrusting t thigh level.

11 c

11 d

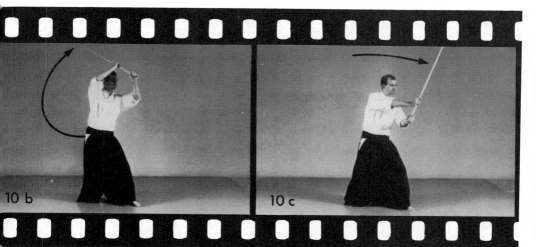

10 b

10 c

11 a

11 b

Movement 12

(12a) In a clockwise direction, move the tip of the jo in a small circle, pulling it back as you do,

12 a

Continued

then (12b) execute tsuki. The size of the circle you describe with the tip of the jo should be about a foot in diameter.

12 b

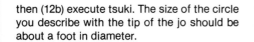

13 b

13 c

Movement 14

(14a) Reach to the far end of the jo and (14b&14c) execute ushiro tsuki. Slide to your rear half a stance length as you make this thrust.

14 a

Movement 13

(13a) Draw the jo back again and (13b&13c) perform *jodan gaeshi* (upper level reversal), simultaneously retracting your left foot back to your right. (13d&13e) Step forward with the right foot and strike with shomen uchi.

13 a

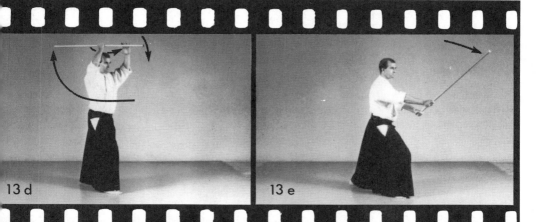

13 d

13 e

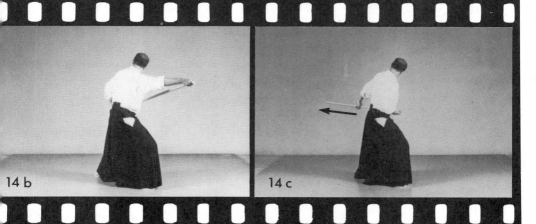

14 b

14 c

Continued

Movement 15

(15a-15c) Step forward with your right foot and execute gedan barai uchi.

15 a

Movement 16

(16a) Cant the far end of the jo down and in a continuous motion, (16b) sweep it up to perpendicular, and then (16c) around to your front, (16d) reversing the ends of the jo. This shift in grip and ends of the jo demands just the right combination of interia and dexterity. Practice it slowly until it is comfortable. The left foot is drawn back during the reversal to a position of regular length sankakudai.

16 a

16 d

Movement 17

(17a) Slide both hands outward to the ends of the jo, holding it parallel to the ground, and (17b) step out with your left foot to execute tsuki.

15 b

15 c

16 b

16 c

17 a

17 b

Continued

Movement 18

(18a) Leave the left foot in place. (18b) Step forward with your right foot, (18c&18d) reversing the jo and (18e&18f) striking with naname barai uchi. (18g&18h) During the sweep, drop down to your left knee. Note (18i&18j) the way the left hand shifts over to accommodate the movement of the jo.

18 a

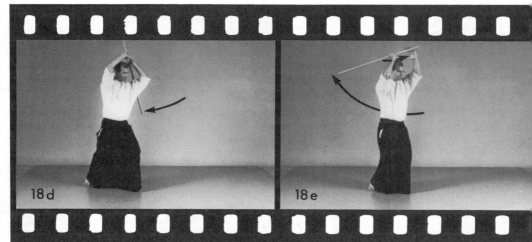

18 d

18 e

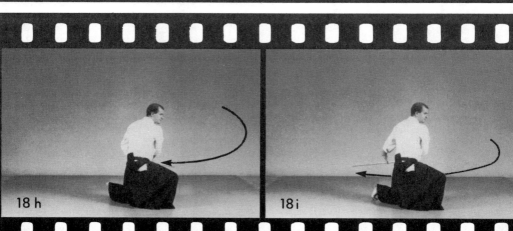

18 h

18 i

18 b

18 c

18 f

18 g

18 j

Continued

Movement 19

(19a&19b) Stand. (19c&19d) Draw your left foot to a position even with your right, and draw the jo around to the right side of your body, pulling it with your right hand to slide it through your left until both hands are at opposite ends. (19e) Step forward, executing ketsugo tsuki.

19 a

19 d

19 e

20 b

20 c

Movement 20

(20a-20c) Reverse the jo and your grip on it, and slide your left foot forward, (20c&20e) executing honte tsuki.

Movement 21

(21a) Widen your grip on the jo by sliding your left hand forward. (21b-21e) Rotate the tip of the jo in a counterclockwise circle. This circle drawn in the air with the jo is about two feet in diameter.

21 a

21 d

21 e

Movement 23

(23a) Lower the jo and (23b) execute honte tsuki.

23 a

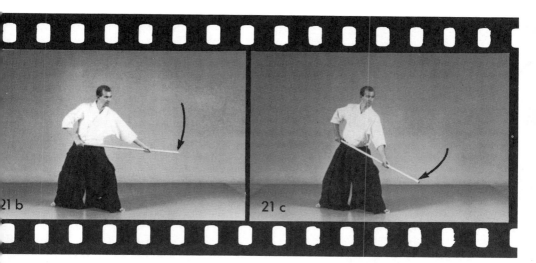

21 b

21 c

Movement 22

(22) Pull the jo back with your right hand and reach with your left until both hands are at opposite ends of the weapon.

22 a

3 b

Continued

Movement 24

(24a) Reach for the far end of the jo with your left hand, pulling the near end back simultaneously with your right hand. (24b&24c) Slide to the rear to execute ushiro tsuki.

24 a

Movement 25

(25a) Swing the jo around from your right side, (25b&25c) stepping forward with your right foot and striking with gedan barai uchi.

25 a

Movement 26

(26a&26b) Raise the jo to chin height on the left side of your body, pulling the near end back with your left hand and allowing the jo to slide through your right until the far end is in your right hand. Then (26c) execute gyakute tsuki. This thrust should be at the level of the opponent's throat.

26 a

24 b

24 c

25 b

25 c

26 b

26 c

Continued

Movement 27

(27a&27b) Slide your right hand out on the jo, pulling back with your left, maintaining the jo in a horizontal position as it is lifted to near jodan level. Step further out with your right foot, (27c) switching grips with your right hand, and (27d&27e) execute shomen uchi.

27 a

27 d

27 e

28 b

Movement 29

(29a&29b) Drive forward with a deep honte tsuki, stepping with your right foot.

27 b

27 c

Movement 28

(28a&28b) Immediately retract your right leg into a bent position off the ground until your right heel touches the inner thigh of your left leg. Pull the near end of the jo deeply to your left side but do not change the grip on it. Movements 28 and 29 are called *nami gaeshi* (a wave's return) which calls to mind the wave-like roll of the legs and body. Raising the leg must be done with all possible speed and power as it is intended to avoid an attack.

28 a

29 a

29 b

Continued

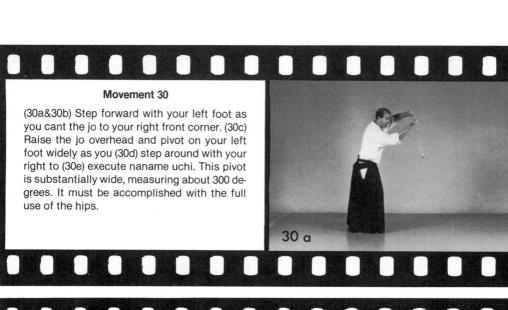

Movement 30

(30a&30b) Step forward with your left foot as you cant the jo to your right front corner. (30c) Raise the jo overhead and pivot on your left foot widely as you (30d) step around with your right to (30e) execute naname uchi. This pivot is substantially wide, measuring about 300 degrees. It must be accomplished with the full use of the hips.

30 a

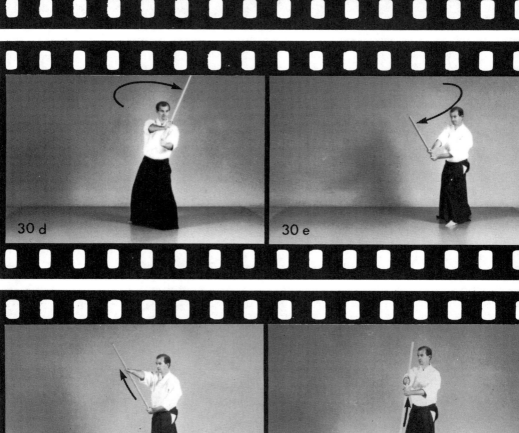

30 d

30 e

31 b

31 c

O b

30 c

Movement 31

(31a) Pause, then (31b&31c) tilt the jo upward, sliding both hands to its middle. (31d&31e) Lower the jo's distal tip to the ground and pivot back around to face the direction in which you began the exercise. Lower your right hand to your side; slide your left hand upward on the jo, returning to your original position. This concludes the 31-count tandoku renshu for the jo.

31 a

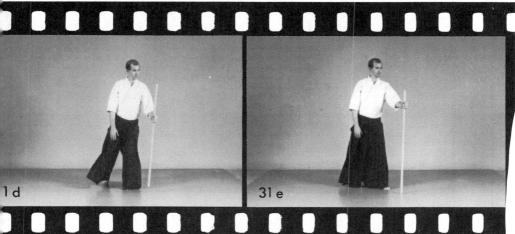

1 d

31 e

RENSHU BUNKAI
(ANALYSIS OF MAJOR TECHNIQUES)

In this concluding chapter we examine, in a cursory way, some of the meanings behind the tandoku renshu—their bunkai. Some of these will be obvious; others may come as a surprise: all of them are evidence of the impressive knowledge and skills of the early masters who created the exercise.

Nearly all techniques in this exercise are applied against a swordsman. This is only natural, since virtually all of the Japanese martial disciplines of old were directed at defeating a sword-carrying opponent. It should be the budoka's primary concern to learn to use the jo as it was originally intended. When that is thoroughly attained, he may then improvise at will.

The analysis of techniques, whether they occur in a simple waza, a tandoku waza, a tandoku renshu, or a kata, is a fascinating study. It is a matter of going behind immediate appearances, going deeper than the obvious, to discover the subtle; to explore an area normally hidden to some extent. It is a formidable undertaking for the budoka. He must be willing to forego his own interpretations and ideas and absorb with an open mind the instructions of his teachers. And when their knowledge has been exhausted, he must investigate what exponents of the past found in the techniques. Finally, after nearly a lifetime of training, if he's fortunate, he may begin to find new and different meanings still in the movements. In the old, he will recognize the new. The implications of this wisdom go far beyond the realm of training.

Editor's Note: The applications to Movements 5, 7, 12, 22, 23 and 31 are not illustrated in this chapter because these particular movements apply only to very elementary combat techniques easily discerned just from the exercise itself. Movement 5, for instance, has only one purpose, *naname uchi;* Movements 12, 22, and 23 are simple thrusts; and Movement 31 is only a formal way of closing the exercise. It has no combat applications.

In the *yoi*, or beginning position, although the practitioner is stationary, his kamae allows immediate and effective movement against the opponent. He may respond with: *ago tsuki* (thrust to the chin); *gyaku tate uchi* (reverse vertical strike) to the jaw or throat, or *katate gyaku tsuki* (one handed reverse thrust) to the opponent's bicep, rendering him incapable of correctly drawing his weapon.

Ago Tsuki
(Thrust to the Chin)

(1) From the beginning position, (2) step in quickly with your left foot toward the swordsman, and drive the near end of the jo upward under his chin.

Movement 1 may be employed as *soto uke* (outer parry) against a thrust. It may be also a *soto harai* (outside reap) against the opponent's left. These actions may also serve as *naname barai uke* (oblique angular parry) against a thrust, followed by a tsuki.

**Gyaku Tate Uchi
(Reverse Vertical Strike)**

(1) From the beginning position, (2) step forward with your left foot, and swing the far end of the jo upward to strike the swordsman in his jaw or throat.

Katate Gyaku Tsuki (One Handed Reverse Thrust)

(1) From the beginning position, (2) step forward with your left foot, swing the far end of the jo upward into position, then drive it forward into the swordsman's bicep.

Soto Uke
(Outer Parry)

(1) From the beginning position (2) as the swordsman thrusts for your throat, grip the jo with both hands, and parry the sword thrust away from your body to the right side.

Soto Harai
(Outside Reap)

(1) From the beginning position, (2) step diagonally forward with your right foot to your right front corner and towards the swordsman's left side. (3) Grip the jo with both hands. (4) Swing the far end out in a circle as you continue to move forward. (5) As you continue your momentum, begin to step with your left foot and bring the jo back to catch the back of the swordsman's legs behind his knees. Then (6&7) drive the jo back forcefully to break his stance as you (8) step forward with your left foot and drop to your right knee to bring him down.

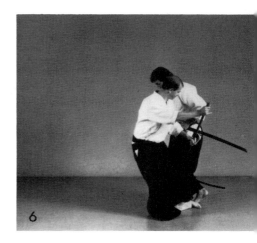

2

4

5

7

8

Naname Barai Uke
(Oblique Angular Parry)

(1) From the beginning position, (2) as the swordsman steps forward with a thrust, grip the jo with both hands and deflect the sword thrust by swinging the far end of the jo outward. This not only parries the thrust side, but also positions the jo for a

follow-up. (3) Pull the jo back on your right side with your right hand, sliding it through your left until the far end comes back into your left hand. Then (4) step forward as you execute a thrust of your own to the swordsman's solar plexus.

Movement 2 may be used as *age uchi* (a rising strike) to attack the swordsman's grip. Combined with Movement 3 it can become *naname age uke* (an oblique upward parry) succeeded by a thrust to the solar plexus.

**Age Uchi
(Rising Strike)**

(1) As the swordsman strikes down with shomen uchi, (2) use Movement 2 to drive the jo upward, striking his grip on the sword. The force of your upward strike to the swordsman's hands is enhanced by their downward motion.

Naname Age Uchi (Oblique Upward Parry)

(1&2) As the swordsman strikes down with shomen uchi, use Movement 2 to block, bringing your left foot back and swerving it to the right side as you raise the jo. This not only blocks the strike but also angles you out of his line of strike. Then (3) drive forward, stepping with your left foot, and thrusting to his solar plexus.

129

Jodan gaeshi, the upper level reversal, which occurs throughout the 31-count tandoku renshu can have many applications. Among them is naname age uchi, the oblique upward parry against shomen uchi, with a counterstrike.

The second part of this movement is obviously a diagonal strike with the jo, but it may also be *shiho nage* (four corners throw) used to fell an opponent who has seized the far end of the jo.

**Naname Age Uchi
(Oblique Upward Parry)**

(1&2) As the swordsman strikes down with shomen uchi, raise the jo to execute the block, both hands in the middle of the jo. (3) Step toward the swordsman with your right foot as you rotate

the jo clockwise with your right hand, (4) releasing your left hand, grip the other end of the jo as it comes around. Then strike with naname uchi.

Shiho Nage
(Four Corners Throw)

(1-3) To counter an opponent who grabs the far end of the jo in an attempt to wrest control of the weapon from you, move forward and raise the jo as if executing na-

name uchi. (4) Step forward and follow through with the naname uchi movement, thus unbalancing your opponent and throwing him.

3

4

In Movement 6, a similar form of shiho nage as was applied in Movement 4 may be implemented against an opponent's grip, pivoting 180 degrees this time to gather momentum for the throw.

Shiho Nage
(Four Corners Throw)

(1&2) To counter an opponent who grabs the other end of the jo, (3) pivot 180 degrees to your right on your left foot, swinging your right foot around behind you, then (4-7) drive the jo down diagonally as though executing naname uchi. This movement breaks your opponent's balance and throws him to the ground.

2

4

5

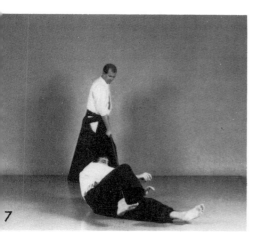

7

The broad, horizontal strike of *yoko barai uchi* (side sweep) performed with a pivot may demonstrate an example of threatening an opponent to keep him at bay and allow a readjustment of your distancing. Hidden within the pivot is a method too, of throwing an attacker who has taken hold of you from behind—*ushiro ryokata-dori kokyu nage* (two handed breath throw).

1

**Yoko Barai Uchi
(Side Sweep Strike)**

(1&2) Sensing the approach of a swordsman from behind, (3) pivot quickly on the balls of both feet, and drop to one knee as you swing the jo in a wide horizontal

2

arc. To avoid the strike, the swordsman is forced to stop his advance or even shift back, thus (5) giving you the opportunity to face him and adjust your distance.

Ushiro Ryokata-Dori Kokyu Nage (Two Handed Breath Throw)

(1&2) As your opponent grabs you in a bear hug from behind, (3) counter by pivoting quickly 180 degrees to the right, just as though executing the wide horizontal

sweep. This movement (4) throws the opponent so that (5) he lands in front of you, vulnerable to a follow-up technique.

The age uchi of Movements 9 and 10 may be employed against the swordsman's grip on his weapon.

It may also be interpreted as *juji garami nage* (entangling throw), a method of inserting the jo between the swordsman's grip, pinning him, and then following through with the jo as if striking down to execute the throw.

Movements 9 and 10 may emerge too as a *dome* (block) against the swordsman's shomen uchi, followed by a strike to the outer elbow, the rib area, or the neck.

**Juji Garami Nage
(Entangling Throw)**

(1&2) As the swordsman steps forward with shomen uchi, drive the jo upward just as if executing age uchi, but instead of striking his hands, insert the far end of the jo between his wrists. Your right foot is forward. (3)

Step forward with your left foot, lifting the jo as though preparing to strike. (4) Drive the jo diagonally downward as though executing naname uchi and (5) throw the swordsman to the ground.

Dome
(Block)

(1&2) As the swordsman strikes down with shomen uchi, step forward with your right foot, turning your hips, and driving the jo upward between his wrists. (3) Step with your right foot toward your left front corner and sweep the jo in that direction. Your force is perpendicular to the imaginary line connecting the swordsman's heels. This (4) breaks his balance and topples him backward. (5) As he tries to recover, (6) step in toward him with your left foot, and (7) strike with naname uchi to his elbow. His ribs and his neck are also available targets from this position.

2

4

5

7

The initial part of this movement may be a way to retract the jo in preparation for a thrust, but within its action is a technique against the opponent who has grasped the jo. This response is nearly identical to *nikkyo,* the second form of pinning in aikido, and it should be performed with that in mind.

In addition, this movement is a form of *go no sen,* inducing an opponent into attack by offering an opening and then countering.

Nikkyo
(Second Pinning Principle)

(1&2) When your opponent grabs the other end of the jo in an attempt to gain control, (3&4) grip the far tip of the jo, and (5&6) position it over his wrist. Then (7) push downward to bring the opponent to his knees.

Go No Sen
(Setting Up the Opponent for a Counter)

(1) Get set in the ready position, close enough to the swordsman that he needs only take one step to come within striking distance. (2) As he steps forward to execute shomen uchi, step back with your back leg, and slide your front foot back as well, shifting your body out

of range. Simultaneously reach for the far end of the jo with your left hand as you pull it back with your right. (3) The swordsman hesitates in his strike in response to your shifting beyond his range. (4) In that instant, lunge forward and thrust to his midsection.

The upper level reversal is repeated in Movement 13. In this application, jodan gaeshi followed by shomen uchi, are used as an *irimi* (entering) form for *shiho nage* (four directions throw).

Shiho Nage
(Four Directions Throw)

(1&2) As your opponent grabs the far end of the jo, (3) step forward, and (4&5) pivot to your right, bringing the jo to the jodan level, and sliding your left hand next to your right. (6) As you continue to pivot, release your left hand and shift it to grip the other end of the jo, thus effecting the reversal. (7) Step back with your left foot as you complete the 180-degree pivot, and (8) drive the jo downward as though executing shomen uchi. This breaks the opponent's balance, and (9) brings him down to the ground.

Movement 14, which places the jo in waki kamae, should not be thought of as a defensive position. It permits the jo to be used at a much closer distance, executing *tsuki* (thrust) with the near tip, for instance.

Withdrawing the jo and the body may be implemented as another means to set up an attack by providing an apparent opening and then countering with *gedan barai uchi* (lower level sweep strike) as the opponent steps in.

These movements may also be interpreted as a technique for offering the jo to an opponent at the rear, then throwing him with a *kokyu nage* (breath throw).

Gedan Barai Uchi
(Lower Level Sweep Strike)

(1) As the swordsman prepares to strike, reach for the far end of the jo with your right hand as you step back with your left foot. (2) As he begins to strike, shift back out of range and slide the jo into waki kamae to the rear. (3) As he tries to recover in response to your shifting out of range, drive forward and strike with gedan barai uchi.

Tsuki
(Thrust)

(1) With your jo in waki kamae, the swordsman prepares to strike with sho-men uchi. (2) As he steps forward with his downward cut, drive toward him into a kneeling position (3) past the cutting plane of the sword. At this point if he manages to follow through with his cut, the blade of the sword will not touch you. Then, thrust with the near tip into his midsection.

Kokyu Nage
(Breath Throw)

(1&2) As you position the jo in waki kame just within a distance which necessitates his reaching forward to grab it. At this time, your back foot is already firmly planted. (3&4) Turn sharply to execute the gedan barai uchi movement. The circular path of the jo will break his

balance as he attempts to move forward quickly. (5&6) Continue to turn in a tight pivot, turning your whole body, and swinging your back leg around to the front to complete the movement and throw the opponent to the ground.

Upon first examination, this action appears nothing more than a way of retracting the jo after a strike and reversing the ends to prepare for another attack. With proper understanding, however, a variety of levels of application are brought to light. Among them: *gaeshi tsuki* (reversal thrust) used as a method of felling an opponent who has gripped the jo from a low level, and using the following thrust of Movement 17 to attack his kidneys or spine.

One variation of this gaeshi tsuki is to use it simply as a means to escape the opponent's grasp, and then to follow with a counterthrust.

Another variation is to use this movement as a countering tsuki at close range.

Movement 16 may also be *uke nagashi tsuki,* a parry against the swordsman's thrust followed by a counterthrust in Movement 17 at his inner thigh.

Gaeshi Tsuki
(Reversal Thrust)

(1) The opponent grabs the other end of the jo which is in a low position. As soon as he establishes a firm grip but before he can establish a stable stance, (2&3) step forward into a strong stance and perform the reversal movement. This pulls the

other end of the jo down and back, and drags the opponent off balance. (4) As he falls continue the reversal, pulling the jo from his grasp. (5) Reverse ends, and finish the opponent with a final thrust.

Kazure Gaeshi Tsuki: 1 (Variation of Reversal Thrust: 1)

(1) The opponent reaches forward and grabs the middle of the jo. (2) Begin the reversal movement before he has a chance to establish a strong stance. (3&4) The re-

versal movement locks his wrist and pulls him forward, forcing him to (5) release his grip as you complete the reversal. (6) Counter with a final thrust to the groin.

**Kazure Gaeshi Tsuki: 2
(Variation of Reversal
Thrust: 2)**

(1) The opponent reaches forward and grabs the middle of the jo. (2) Begin the reversal movement to lock his wrist and pull him forward. (3) The opponent's grip is loosened but he does not let go. Instead, he shifts for-

ward to regain his balance and relieve the stress on his wrist. (4) Continue the reversal movement but before completing it, step forward, and drive the near end of the tip into his neck.

Uke Nagashi Tsuki
(Flowing Parry and Thrust)

(1&2) As the swordsman thrusts, begin the reversal movement, swinging the far end of the jo down and back, and parry the sword out-

ward with the jo. (3&4) Complete the reversal of the jo, and (5) counter with a thrust to the swordsman's inner thigh.

An alternative application for the tsuki is demonstrated, sliding the jo alongside the swordsman's leg, scooping it up and throwing him in *sukui otoshi* (scooping drop).

**Sukui Otoshi
(Scooping Drop)**

(1) Facing the swordsman, (2) step forward with your left foot, and slide the jo across the inside of his forward leg. (3) Pivot to your right on your left foot, swinging your right hand be-

hind you, and hook the jo around the back of the swordsman's leg. (4&5) Follow through by scooping the jo forward and up to throw the swordsman on his back.

Naname uchi against a middle level target may be utilized as a technique for attacking a threatening swordsman, striking against his left hand before he can unsheathe his blade.

The same movement can be employed as a *surukomi uchi* (sliding strike) to dash away an opponent's weapon or break it. Utilizing the change in the grip, this movement can be continued as a tsuki to the swordsman's solar plexus.

Movement 18 can also be a method for avoiding a strike aimed at your body by dropping down and countering with a strike to the opponent's inner thigh.

Naname Uchi
(Diagonal Strike)

Movement 18 can be used to execute a preemptive strike against the swordsman. (1) Facing the swordsman, (2-4) execute the upper level reversal, and (5&6) strike down with naname uchi to (7) strike his hand before he has the chance to draw the sword. With his left hand injured, the swordsman's ability to wield the sword effectively is seriously impaired.

2

4

5

7

165

Surukomi Uchi
(Sliding Strike)

(1) Facing the swordsman, Movement 18 can be used to clear the way for a preemp-

tive strike. (2-5) Execute the upper level reversal, and

167

Continued

(6&7) strike down against the sword with naname uchi. Upon contact with the back of the sword, the jo crosses it such that the far end slants to the right side. (8) As you follow through, the jo slides along the sword, imparting its force

primarily downward at first, but then finally against the right side of the sword, dashing down and out to the left. (9) Grip the jo with both hands, and (10) drive the near tip into the swordsman's midsection.

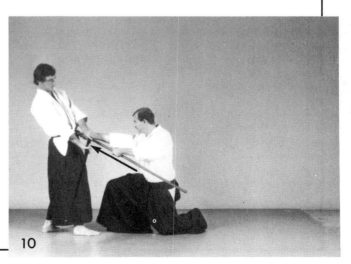

1

Kaeshi Uchi Mata Ate (Counterstrike to Inner Thigh)

(1&2) As the swordsman attacks with a side strike, execute the upper level reversal, and (3&4) drop low to one

2

knee following through with
naname uchi to the groin as
the sword passes over your
head.

It is possible to use this movement as a way of side-stepping a swordsman's shomen uchi and simultaneously moving in close enough to attack with a thrust.

**Sumi Nagashi Tsuki Migi
(Evading Right Corner
Thrust)**

(1&2) As the swordsman begins to strike down with shomen uchi, rise to a standing position, moving forward and turning to the right side. (3) Pivot to the right on your right foot, swinging your left foot around to the front to (4)

turn your left side to the swordsman, pull the jo back into position, and shift to the right line of strike. (5) Execute the thrust to his chest as his strike misses to the left.

Once again an application is concealed within an outwardly innocuous form. Reversing the jo allows the exponent to dash aside a thrust *soto maki uke* (outer wrapping parry) and to return with a counterthrust.

**Soto Maki Uke
(Outer Wrapping Parry)**

(1&2) As the swordsman steps forward with a thrust for your midsection, use the reversal movement to position the jo for a parry of the

3

sword to the left. (3&4) Complete the reversal of the jo, and then (5) counter with a thrust to the swordsman's chest.

4

5

As was explained in Movement 12, this motion with the jo serves as *nikkyo,* a pinning technique against an opponent's wrist.

**Nikkyo
(Second Pinning Principle)**

(1) The opponent grabs the far end of the jo. (2) Widen your grip on the jo by sliding your left hand forward. This gives you more leverage. Then (3) rotate the tip of the jo upward to (4) position it

over the opponent's wrist. Grip the end of the jo, and (5) press down with the jo, dropping to one knee to bring the opponent down to the ground.

Reaching forward with the jo may be used to attack or threaten an opponent's face, disorienting him in terms of distancing and forestalling his attack long enough to allow a *gedan barai uchi* (lower level sweep strike) to his inner knee.

Movement 25 is also a technique for upending an attacker with a version of *sukui otoshi* (scooping drop).

**Gedan Barai Uchi
(Lower Level Sweep Strike)**

(1) As the swordsman raises the sword for a strike, shift in and reach forward toward his face. This will cause him to hestitate in his strike. (2&3) Slide back and perform the ushiro tsuki move-

ment. Then (4&5) swing the jo around, turning to your left as you step forward with your right foot and strike to the swordsman's knee with gedan barai uchi.

1

**Sukui Otoshi
(Scooping Drop)**

(1) With the jo at the rear in waki kamae, (2) the opponent reaches forward the grab your lapel. (3) Step forward with your right foot, turning your hips and swing-

2

ing the jo around the right side to (4) hook behind the opponent's legs. (5) Continue the movement to sweep his legs from under him and bring him down.

Raising the jo and striking with a thrust is a technique for smashing at the sword hilt and wrists of a swordsman and following through with the counter.

**Kobushi Ate no Tsuki
(Strike Fist and Thrust)**

(1) As the swordsman raises his sword and (2) begins to strike down with shomen uchi, raise the far end of the jo, and (3) strike upward to

his wrists as they come down. This will halt his strike. (4) Follow up with a thrust to the chest.

These movements include a wide shomen uchi to slash down against an opponent's sword, knocking it aside or breaking it, and a driving tsuki which follows immediately.

Nami Gaeshi Tsuki ("Returning Wave" Thrust)

(1&2) As the swordsman steps forward with a thrust for your midsection, strike down hard with shomen uchi to (3) knock it aside. If your blow is hard enough it

may even break the sword. (4) Execute the nami gaeshi (a wave's return) movement, and (5&6) drive forward with a thrust to the swordsman's chest.

This strike, which is performed as the body pivots in a semicircle, serves as a method of escaping a strike and delivering a counter.

However, it may also be employed against a seizing of the jo to throw the opponent.

**Naname Uke no
Naname Uchi
(Oblique Block and
Oblique Strike)**

(1&2) The swordsman steps forward and begins to strike down with shomen uchi. Step forward with your left foot as you cant the jo to the right. (3) Pivot to the right on your left foot to take

yourself out of his line of strike. (4) Continue to pivot as you circle the jo overhead, and (5) as you swing your right leg around behind you, strike down with naname uchi.

Jo Dori Sumi Otoshi
(Corner Drop Throw Against a Jo Seizure)

(1&2) The opponent grabs the far end of the jo. Move forward, (3) stepping forward with your left foot, and (4) cant the jo to the right as you begin to pivot to the right on your left foot. This action raises the opponent on his toes as he attempts to hold on to the jo. (5) Continue to pivot and swing the jo around the right side, sweeping your right leg back behind you. This leverage topples the opponent (6) to the ground. (7) Finish him with a thrust to the head.

5

GLOSSARY

Age—A prefix form of the verb *ageru,* and meaning to rise.

Barai—A verb meaning to sweep or to reap. Also pronounced as *harai.*

Bunkai—An analysis of technique; an explanation or an understanding of the elements within a technique or a series of movements.

Chudan—Middle level.

Do—A path or Way. In Japanese, *do* refers to any of several disciplines designed to train the practitioner in technical skills which have as their ultimate goal, the perfection of the spirit.

Dome—A verb meaning to block or arrest a motion.

Gaeshi—A reversal; to pivot or rotate.

Gedan—Lower level.

Gyakute—The reverse hand or opposite hand.

Hanbo—A shorter stick than the jo, usually measuring about 90 centimeters. Also referred to as a *tanjo.*

Handachi—Half-standing literally; kneeling, usually with one knee on the ground and the other raised.

Hanmi—Half-facing. The oblique stance taken in many martial arts and Ways.

Happo—Eight directions. The word often indicates by extension all directions.

Harai—A verb meaning to sweep or to reap. Also pronounced as *barai.*

Hidari—Left direction.

Honte—True hand or basic hand. The term usually refers to a basic method of gripping or holding.

Jiku ashi—The pivot leg upon which one's weight rests at the completion of a pivotal change in direction.

Jo—The Japanese staff, usually measuring about 130 centimeters.

Jodan—Upper level.

Jodo—The budo form devoted to the study of the jo.

Jojutsu—The bujutsu form devoted to the art of the jo.

Juji garami—Figure-ten entanglement. This refers to a number of arm pins or entanglements in which the arms of the opponent are twisted to form roughly the Japanese written character for ten, which resembles a plus (+).

Kamae—A posture which reflects combative spirit.

Kata—A form or series of formalized movements used for training in the martial arts and Ways. The term may also refer to methods or techniques, as in *uchikata* (striking methods).

Keikogi—The training uniform, typically consisting of pants and a jacket, a wide belt and split skirt *(hakama)*.

Ketsugo—A combination of two different methods. When the jo is held with one fist pointing up and the other down, it is referred to as a ketsugo grip.

Kihon—Basics or fundamentals.

Kontei—The tip or butt-end of the jo.

Migi—Right direction.

Naname—At an oblique angle.

Nigiri—To grip or to hold.

Osae—A verb meaning to pin.

Renshu—Practice or training.

Renwaku—Combination. Renwaku waza are combination techniques.

Renzoku—A continuation. Renzoku waza are techniques which are repeated in succession.

Sankakudai—A basic stance taken in jo training, with the front foot pointing straight forward and the rear out at slightly less than 90 degrees, which forms a triangle of sorts. This is the position of the feet when the body is in Hanmi.

Shiho—Four directions. This refers to a number of related throwing techniques which, when properly employed, may be used to fell an opponent in any of four or more directions.

Shiho nage—Four directions throw.

Shomen—A directional term meaning to the front. Shomen uchi refers specifically to a cut or strike at the forehead.

Soto maki uke—An outer wrapping parry, in which the jo connects with a target and slides or dashes it to the outside.

Sukui otoshi—Scooping drop, a throw in which the opponent's legs are scooped up and he's dropped to the ground.

Sumi otoshi—Corner drop, a throw in which the opponent's body is directed out at an angle.

Surukomi uchi—A strike in which the blow is slid or pushed, either against an opponent or his weapon.

Tandoku renshu—Solo practice.

Tanjo—Another term for the hanbo.

Tsuki—A thrust.

Uchi—A verb meaning to strike or to hit.

Uke—Although this word is commonly used to mean a block, in proper usage it is a parry. The distinction is that a block *(dome)* interrupts and arrests the flow of an attack, while a parry redirects it.

Waki kamae—A posture with the jo held out to the side and pointing to the rear corner of the exponent.

Waza—Technique.

Yoi—A position or preparation.

Yoko—A term to denote the side or the flank.

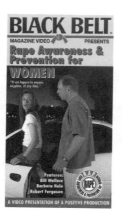

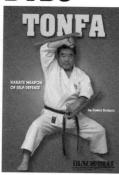

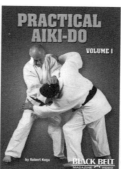
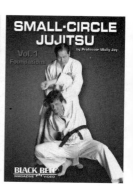